Belwin
Classic
Library

Favorite

RECITAL REPERTOIRE

Selected and Edited by GAIL LEW

24 Piano Pieces
From Four Stylistic Periods

PREFACE

Favorite Recital Repertoire is a collection of authentic keyboard literature for the intermediate pianist who wants to perform brilliant, showy pieces for recitals, special events, or any variety of performance opportunities. The book consists of carefully selected repertoire from the Baroque, Classical, Romantic, and Contemporary periods.

This collection truly represents student favorites, pieces that students through the years have consistently chosen for their special recital piece. This collection features the blockbuster favorites chosen for melodic content, rhythmic vitality, and pianistic flair. Some editorial markings have been added to guide the student in musical style and interpretation. These include pianistic fingerings, stylistic articulations, and carefully placed pedal markings.

GAIL LEW

Gail Lew, clinician, arranger, editor, and piano teacher, is the director of keyboard publications at Warner Bros. Publications in Miami, Florida. Gail has served as senior piano editor for Kjos Music in San Diego, new music reviewer for *California Music Teacher* magazine, and clinician for Frederick Harris Music Company in Toronto. She received her bachelor of music degree in piano performance and continued her graduate studies in music history and literature. Gail is a sought-after presenter and clinician in the United States and Canada and performs yearly at the Music Teachers National Association Convention, many of its state affiliates, and the World Piano Pedagogy Conference.

Gail has received national acclaim for her carefully edited and researched editions of music by Alexandre Tansman, Dmitri Kabalevsky, Samuel Maykapar, Darius Milhaud, Yoshinao Nakada, Robert Starer, Alexander Tcherepnin, and other contemporary composers. She has also written arrangements of popular music for the new *Looney Tunes Piano Library* and *WB Popular Piano Library*, compiled and edited technic books for the *Technic Is Fun* series, and written arrangements of sacred music for the *WB Christian Piano Library*. Gail is an active member of the Music Teachers National Association, the Miami Music Teachers Association, the Broward County Music Teachers Association, and the National Guild of Piano Teachers.

Gail brings more than 20 years of private piano teaching experience to her position as director of keyboard publications and to her interesting and informative sessions on teaching methods, motivating students, and transitioning students from method books to works of master composers.

CONTENTS

MINUET IN G MAJOR

from the Notebook for Anna Magdalena Bach
BWV Anhang 114

CHRISTIAN PETZOLD
(1677-1733)

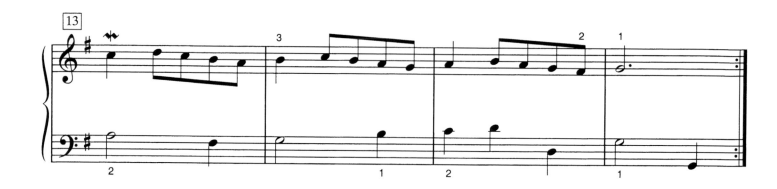

EL03459A

MINUET IN G MINOR

from the Notebook for Anna Magdalena Bach
BWV Anhang 115

CHRISTIAN PETZOLD
(1677-1733)

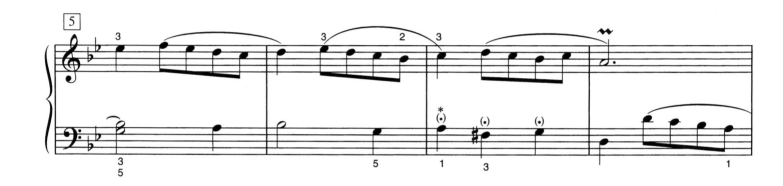

*Phrasing and dynamics are editorial.

EL03459A

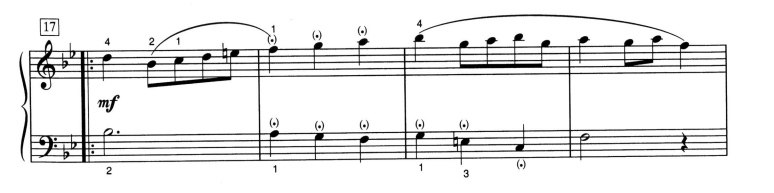

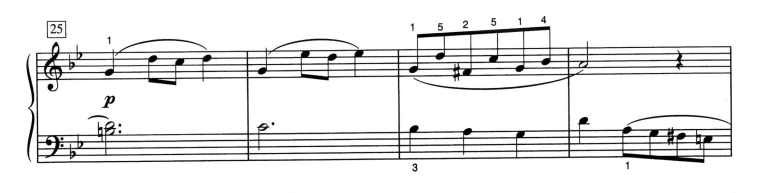

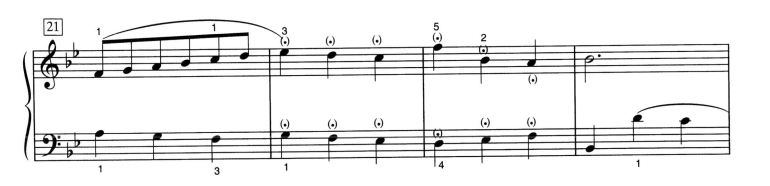

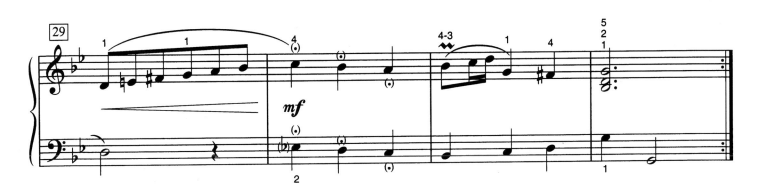

MUSETTE IN D MAJOR

from the Notebook for Anna Magdalena Bach
BWV Anhang 126

ANONYMOUS

*Phrasing, articulation, and dynamic markings are editorial.

MINUET IN G MAJOR

from the Notebook for Anna Magdalena Bach
BWV Anhang 116

ANONYMOUS

*Phrasing, articulation, and dynamic markings are editorial.
**Unarticulated quarter notes may be played legato or non-legato.

*The manuscript is unclear whether this note should be D♮ or D♯.

EL03459A

SONATA IN D MINOR

L. 423

DOMENICO SCARLATTI
(1685-1757)

Aria

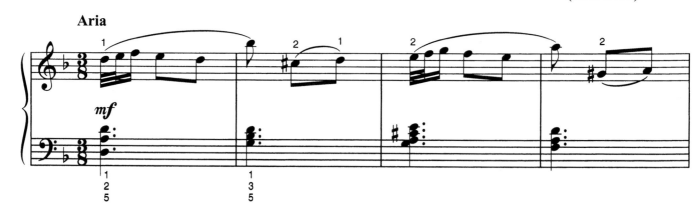

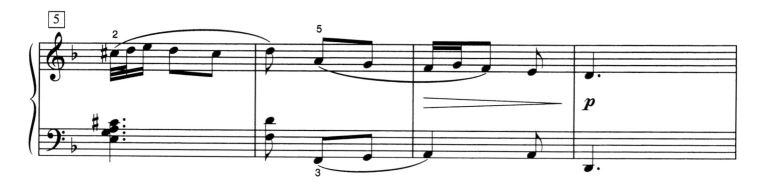

EL03459A

EL03459A

GAVOTA IN D MINOR

K. 64

DOMENICO SCARLATTI
(1685-1757)

*Dynamics, articulations, and fingering indications are editorial.

EL03459A

15

POLONAISE

from the Notebook for Anna Magdalena Bach
BWV Anhang 125

C.P.E. BACH
(1714-1788)

Allegro moderato

*Dynamics, articulations, and fingering indications are editorial.

EL03459A

ALLEGRO IN F MAJOR

FRANZ JOSEPH HAYDN
(1732-1809)

MENUETT

KV 1

WOLFGANG AMADEUS MOZART
(1756-1791)

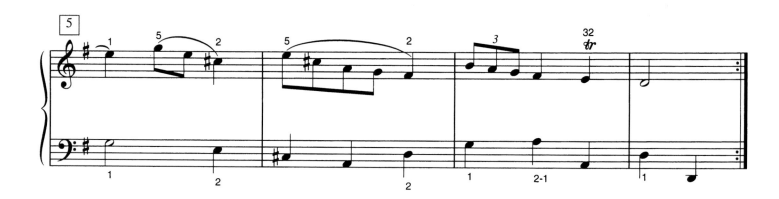

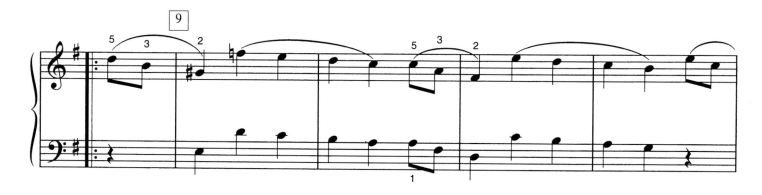

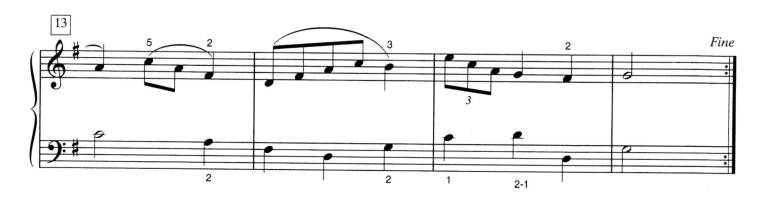

*Phrasing, dynamics, and fingering indications are editorial.

Menuett da capo al Fine

SOLFEGGIETTO*

In C Minor, Wq 117/2

C.P.E. BACH (1714-1788)

*Original title: Solfeggio
**The earliest manuscripts do not indicate any dynamic in measure 1.
***Fingering and pedal indications are editorial. Tempo and dynamics, except as previously indicated, come from the earliest manuscripts.

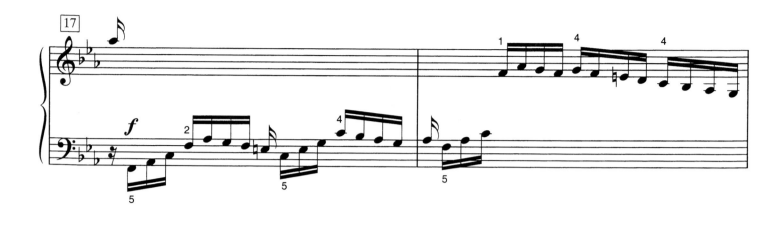

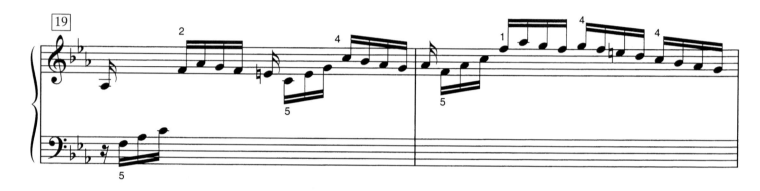

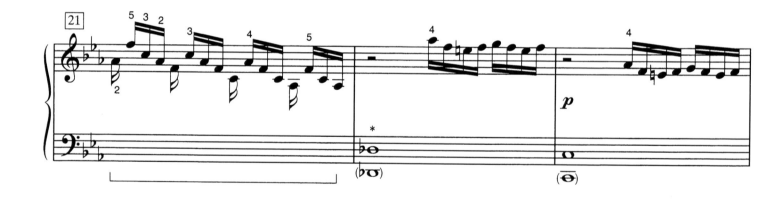

*The notes in parentheses are not present in the earliest manuscripts.

EL03459A

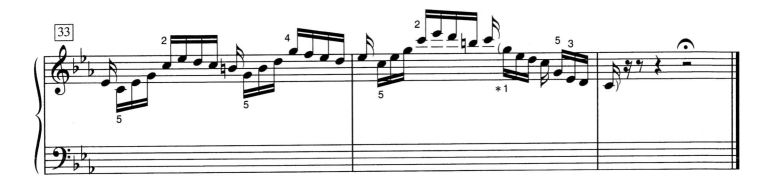

*The earliest manuscripts end the piece with the high C on beat 3.

SONATINA IN A MINOR

GEORG ANTON BENDA
(1722-1795)

*♪ = non legato unless otherwise indicated by slurs.

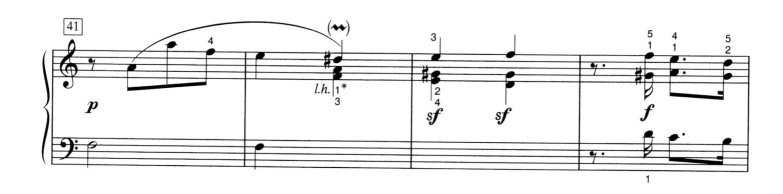

D.C. al Fine

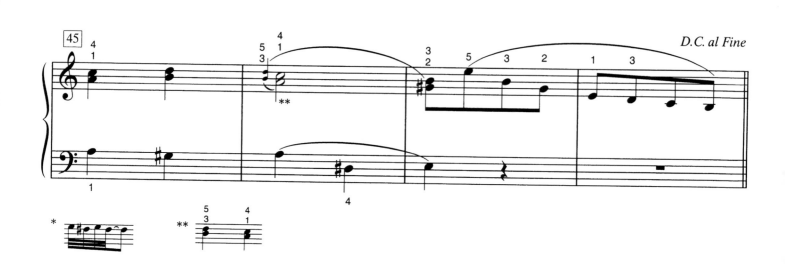

BALLADE

from 25 Etudes, Op. 100, No. 15

FRIEDRICH BURGMÜLLER
(1806-1874)

Allegro con brio (♩. = 66-76)

30

FÜR ELISE
WoO59

LUDWIG van BEETHOVEN
(1770-1827)

Poco moto*

*Although the original edition indicates **Poco molto**, a manuscript sketch by Beethoven has the marking **Molto grazioso**.

EL03459A

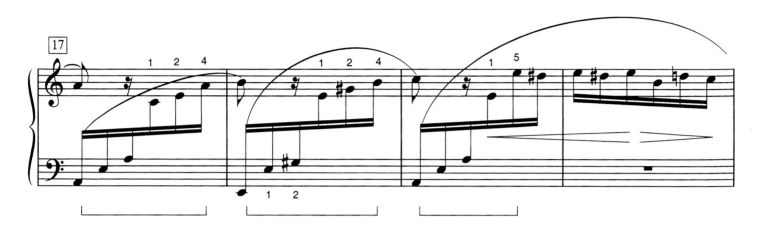

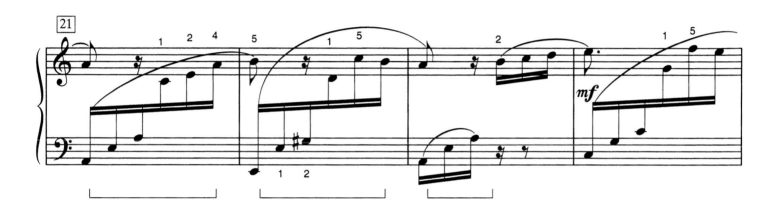

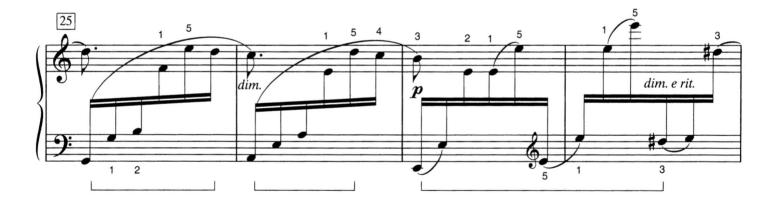

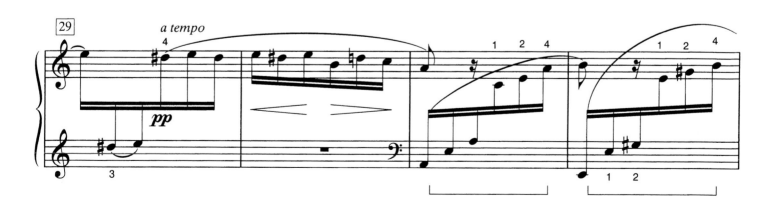

EL03459A

38

EL03459A

ETUDE IN A MINOR

Op. 47, No. 3

STEPHEN HELLER
(1813-1888)

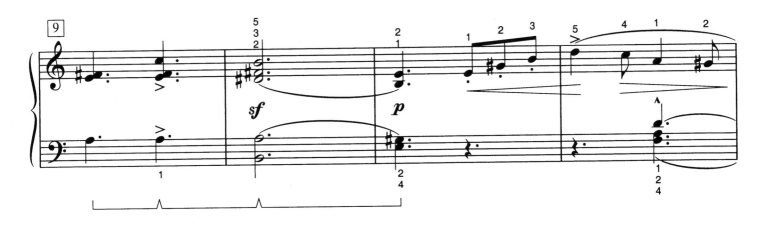

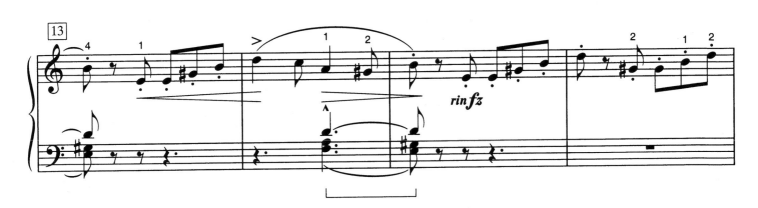

40

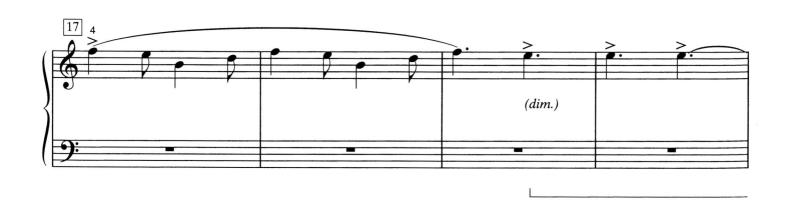

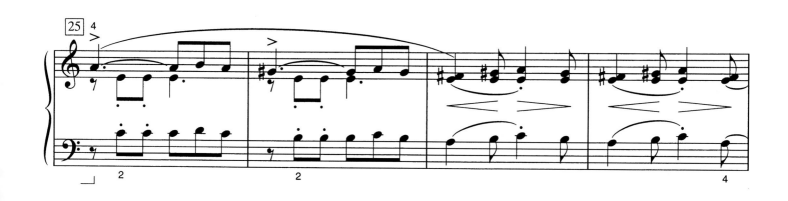

EL03459A

THE AVALANCHE
Op. 45, No. 2

STEPHEN HELLER
(1813-1888)

Allegro vivace

MAZURKA IN G MINOR

Op. 67, No. 2

FRÉDÉRIC CHOPIN
(1810-1849)

*This is Chopin's original tempo. The editor suggests ♩ = ca. 126.
** All pedal markings are editorial.

EL03459A

SPINNING SONG

ALBERT ELLMENREICH
(1816-1905)

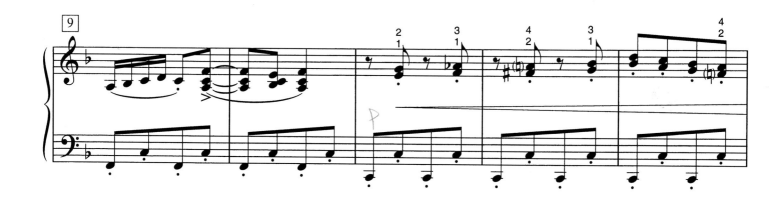

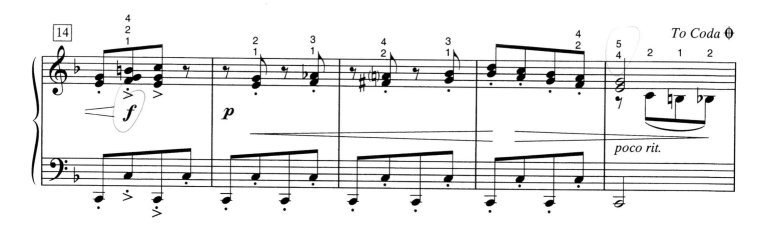

49

EL03459A

WALTZ

from Glass Beads
Op. 123, No. 6

ALEXANDER GRETCHANINOFF
(1864-1956)

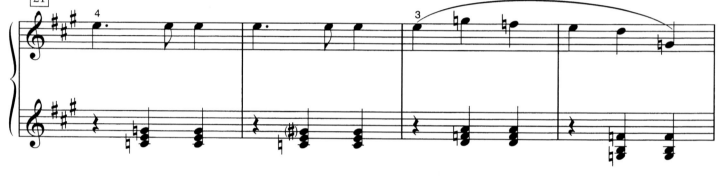

GYMNOPÉDIE
No. 1

ERIK SATIE
(1866-1925)

Très lent (♩ = 96-108)

Una corda and *tre corde* indications are editorial.

57

EL03459A

PRELUDE
No. 19 from Pedal Preludes

SAMUEL MAYKAPAR
(1867-1938)

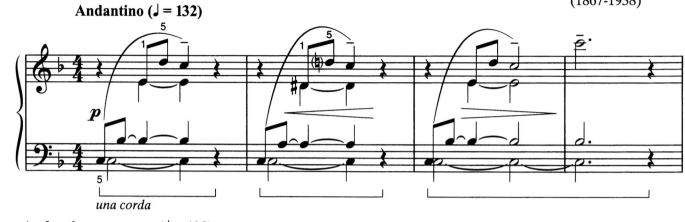

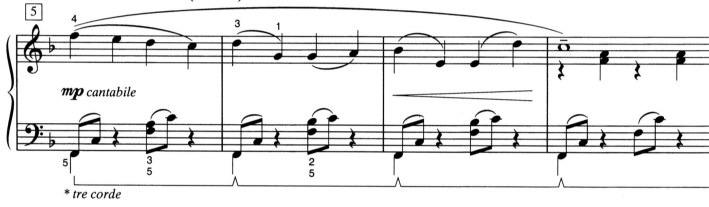

*Maykapar indicated *una corda* throughout the entire piece. *Tre corde* is editorial.

EL03459A

*Editorial phrasing was added in measures 17-25.
**Editorial pedaling was added between counts 1 and 3 in measures 22, 24, 27, 28 and 29.

ETUDE ALLEGRO
from Japanese Festival

YOSHINAO NAKADA
(1923-2000)

*Staccato markings and accents in measures 1, 2, 3 and 4 are editorial.
**Pedal markings are editorial.

EL03459A

*Accent markings in measures 48, 49, and 50 are editorial.

64

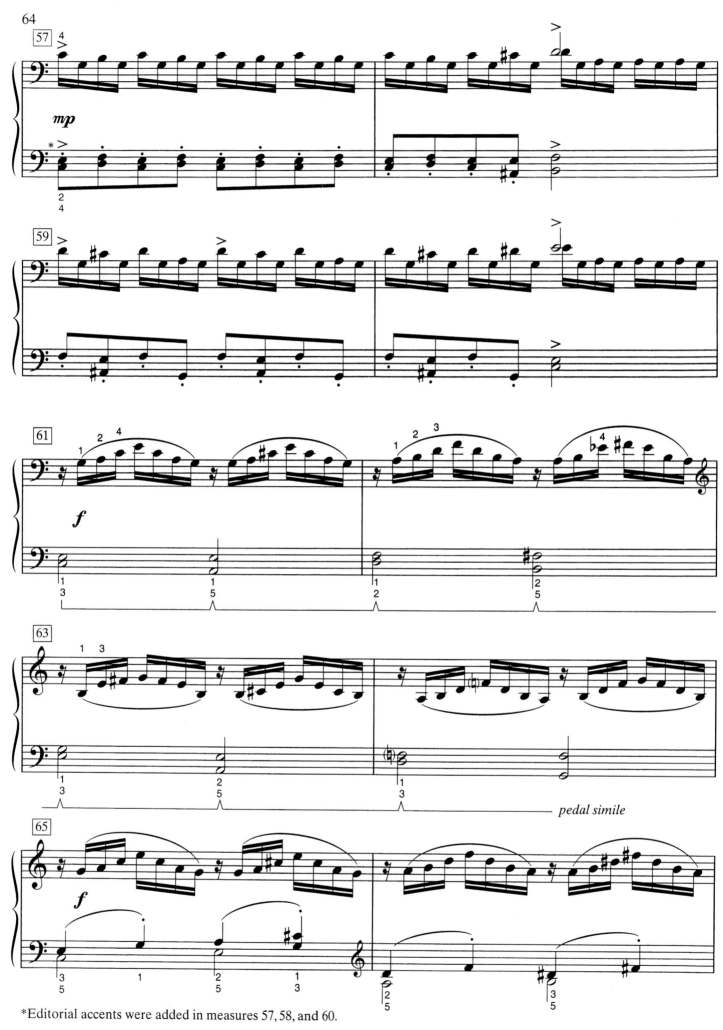

*Editorial accents were added in measures 57, 58, and 60.

IN MEMORY OF
GEORGE GERSHWIN "1925"

from Happy Time Book 3

ALEXANDRE TANSMAN
(1897-1986)

BRIGHT ORANGE

from Sketches in Color, Set 1

ROBERT STARER
(1924-2001)

*Pedal markings are editorial.

70

EL03459A

STRICTLY FOURTHS

from Polytonal Brubeck

DAVE BRUBECK
(1920-   )

1st time (♩ = 88) Very rubato
2nd time (♩ = 120-144)

*Pedal with each chord change.